孔子学院总部 /
国家汉办汉语国际推广成都基地规划教材

走进天府系列教材【成都印象】

梦三国
之蜀国

Dream of the Three Kingdoms: Shu

西 南 财 经 大 学
汉语国际推广成都基地　　著

西南财经大学出版社

中国·成都

西 南 财 经 大 学
汉语国际推广成都基地 著

总策划 涂文涛

策 划
李永强

主 编
梁 婷 白巧燕

编 者
《成都印象·游成都》 胡倩琳
《成都印象·居成都》 郑 莹
《成都印象·吃川菜》 谢 娟 王 新
《成都印象·品川茶》 肖 静
《成都印象·饮川酒》 谢 娟
《成都印象·看川剧》 郑 莹
《成都印象·绣蜀绣》 谢 娟
《成都印象·梦三国之蜀国》 蒋林益 胡佩迦
《成都印象·悟道教》 沙 莎 吕 彦 陈 茉
《成都印象·练武术》 邓 帆 刘 亚

审 订 冯卫东

英文翻译
Alexander Demmelhuber

Introduction

Dream of the Three Kingdoms: Shu is one part of the "Impressions of Chengdu" textbook series, which is promoted by the Chengdu Base of Confucius Institute Headquarters and published by the Southwestern University of Finance and Economics Press. This book contains 8 units, which are designed on the basis of the Confucius Institute Headquarters'/Hanban's "International Curriculum for Chinese Language Education" (hereinafter referred to as "Curriculum"), as can be seen, for example, on vocabulary and language points used, and ensures that this textbook is held to scientific, systematic and rigorous standards.

This book introduces the history and culture of the Three Kingdoms in Chengdu, the heroic stories of the Three Kingdoms and the historical Three Kingdoms sites in Chengdu. It provides students of Chinese with a basic understanding of the Three Kingdoms culture as well as language and background information for visiting the historical sites.

This book is mainly composed of vocabulary and grammar items as can be found in the Curriculum for levels 5 to 6, with some commonly used set phrases, proverbs and two-part allegorical sayings. We hope that this book will help intermediate and advanced students of Chinese to improve their proficiency and deepen their knowledge about history and culture.

Hopefully, you will enjoy *Dream of the Three Kingdoms: Shu*, and we are looking forward to any criticism or suggestions you might have. Hanban gave us much help and support during editing of this book and we would like to take this opportunity to express our gratitude.

前言

　　《梦三国之蜀国》是汉语国际推广成都基地、西南财经大学推出的"成都印象"系列教材之一。全书共 8 课，以孔子学院总部 / 国家汉办的《国际汉语教学通用课程大纲》为基本编写依据，涉及大纲中的大量词汇、语言点等指标，以保证教材的科学性、系统性和严谨性。本书介绍了成都的三国历史文化、三国英雄人物故事以及遗留在成都的三国遗址等内容，为外国汉语学习者了解三国文化及游览三国遗址提供语言和信息的支持。本书语言材料以大纲中的 5-6 级词汇和语法项目为主，加入了一些生活中常用的成语、俗语以及歇后语，希望能够让中高级水平汉语学习者在提升汉语水平的同时了解中国历史文化。

　　希望您能喜欢《梦三国之蜀国》这本教材，也希望您对本书提出批评和建议。本书的编写得到了国家汉办的大力支持和帮助，在此一并表示感谢。

目录

第一课 【梦回三国】
Lesson 1 【A Dream Back to the Three Kingdoms】

① 《赤壁》 《Chì Bì》
② 《三国演义》 《Sānguó Yǎnyì》
③ 诸葛亮 Zhūgě Liàng
④ 英雄 yīngxióng
⑤ 吸引 xīyǐn
⑥ 影响 yǐngxiǎng
⑦ 智慧 zhìhuì
⑧ 仁义 rényì
⑨ 忠诚 zhōngchéng
⑩ 值得 zhídé

（一）
江一华和文小西准备坐地铁去春熙路逛逛……

江一华：

小西，听说有一部电影非常有意思，叫《赤壁》，讲的是三国时期的故事。你想看吗？

文小西：

好啊！我对三国的故事很感兴趣，以前我看过英文版的《三国演义》，那时就很喜欢诸葛亮。

江一华：

小时候我听爷爷讲过《三国演义》这本小说，觉得三国故事里面的英雄人物很吸引人。爷爷说三国时期的历史文化对中国人的影响很大。

文小西：

有哪些影响呢？

⑪战　胜　zhànshèng
⑫宏　大　hóngdà
⑬微　信　wēixìn

江一华：
比如说三国时期有很多关于英雄的故事：诸葛亮的智慧、刘备的仁义、关羽的忠诚等。这些都值得我们学习。

文小西：
那《赤壁》这部电影是什么内容？

江一华：
我看了介绍，讲的是三国时期的一场著名的战争，最后弱小的一方战胜了强大的一方，场面非常宏大。

文小西：
听你这么一说，我都等不及了。咱们马上用微信订票吧。

江一华：
好啊，就订今天晚上七点半的那一场吧。

文小西：
行，正好吃完晚饭就去。

①震撼人心　zhènhàn-rénxīn
②以弱胜强　yǐruò shèngqiáng
③范　例　　fànlì
④一席之地　yìxí-zhīdì

（二）

江一华：
这部电影确实精彩，战争场面太震撼人心了。

文小西：
太好看了！诸葛亮用智慧战胜了强大的敌人。

江一华：
是的，"赤壁之战"是三国故事里非常重要的一场战争，在世界以弱胜强的对战范例中也占有一席之地。

文小西：
我决定再仔细地读一遍这本小说，认真体会一下三国时期的历史文化。

江一华：
没错。我朋友说现在还出现了各种形式的三国文化热。你还记得"三国杀"吗？

⑤乐不思蜀 　lèbù-sīshǔ
⑥举一反三 　jǔyī-fǎnsān

文小西：
　　当然记得。就是上周中国朋友约我们玩的纸牌游戏。

江一华：
　　对。玩游戏还让我学到了不少成语呢，比如"乐不思蜀"。

文小西：
　　这是什么意思？

江一华：
　　意思是在新的环境中过得很快乐，不想回到以前的环境。

文小西：
　　明白了。现在我在成都生活得挺开心的，不想回国，是这个意思吗？

江一华：
　　你还挺会举一反三的。

①浮 现	fúxiàn
②铁 链	tiěliàn
③挥 动	huīdòng
④号 角	hàojiǎo
⑤浓烟滚滚	nóngyān-gǔngǔn
⑥孙刘联军	Sūn-Liú Liánjūn
⑦曹 军	Cáo Jūn

（小阅读）

江一华和文小西回到了宿舍。这天夜里，江一华躺在床上翻来覆去睡不着，他的脑海里不断浮现出电影《赤壁》里的场景。想着想着，他迷迷糊糊地睡着了。

这时，远处仿佛传来了阵阵鼓声，江一华朝着声音传来的方向走到了江边的一座小山上。他看见很多木头做的巨大战船从远处开过来，船与船之间用铁链连在了一起，船上一排排士兵上下挥动着手里的兵器。这时，突然响起了一阵号角声，空中无数带着火苗的箭飞向江中的战船。战船烧起来了，江面上浓烟滚滚。战船被铁链紧紧连在一起，没办法分开。很快所有的战船都燃起了大火。

"啪"的一声，一支箭掉在了江一华的脚边。他被吓醒了，睁开眼睛，发现自己躺在床上，原来刚刚做了一场梦：赤壁之战，孙刘联军以少胜多、以弱胜强，打败了势力强大的曹军。他要把梦里的这个三国故事讲给老师和同学们听。

[Part 1]
(Jiang Yihua and Wen Xiaoxi are about to take the subway to Chunxi Road for some window shopping)

Jiang Yihua: Xiaoxi, I heard about a really interesting movie called *Battle of Red Cliffs*, telling about a story set in the Three Kingdoms period. Do you want to watch it?

Wen Xiaoxi: Sure! Stories about the Three Kingdoms fascinate me. I read the English version of *The Romance of the Three Kingdoms* and liked Zhuge Liang a lot.

Jiang Yihua: When I was a kid, I listened to my grandpa talk about this novel and found the heroes to be captivating. Grandpa said that the history and culture of the Three Kingdoms have left a big impact on the Chinese.

Wen Xiaoxi: In what way?

Jiang Yihua: For example, there are many heroic stories set in this period: Zhuge Liang's wisdom, Liu Bei's righteousness, and Guan Yu's loyalty, to name just a few, are all worthy of study.

Wen Xiaoxi: So what is the ***Battle of Red Cliffs*** about?

Jiang Yihua: I read an overview; it's about a famous battle of the Three Kingdoms period. In the end, the weaker party defeated the mightier party. What a grand scene!

Wen Xiaoxi: If you put it like that, I can't wait to see it. Let's book a ticket through WeChat right away.

Jiang Yihua: All right! Let's book the show at half past seven tonight.

Wen Xiaoxi: Sure! We'll go right after dinner.

[Part 2]
Jiang Yihua: This movie really was wonderful. The battle scene was incredibly thrilling!

Wen Xiaoxi: The movie was great! Zhuge Liang defeated his mighty foes through his wisdom.

Jiang Yihua: Yep. The "Battle of Red Cliffs" is a very important battle in the Three Kingdoms stories and is a prominent example of all battles where the underdog turns the tide.

Wen Xiaoxi: I've decided to carefully read the novel again and really try to immerse myself in the history and culture of the Three Kingdoms period.

Jiang Yihua: Great idea. My friend said that a cultural fever about the Three Kingdoms has broken out. Do you remember "Legends of the Three Kingdoms"?

Wen Xiaoxi: Of course I do. That's the card game we played with our Chinese friends last week.

Jiang Yihua: Right. Playing games also helped me learn a lot of set phrases, such as "so happy as to forget home and duty".

Wen Xiaoxi: What does it mean?

Jiang Yihua: It means having a good time in a new environment, so much so that you don't want to return to your previous environment.

Wen Xiaoxi: Got it. I'm living a happy life in Chengdu and don't want to go back. Is that what it's supposed to mean?

Jiang Yihua: You really know how to learn by analogy!

(A small reading exercise)
Jiang Yihua and Wen Xiaoxi returned to their dormitory. This night, Jiang Yihua tossed and turned in bed, unable to sleep. The scenes of "Battle of Red Cliffs" constantly came back to his mind for so long that he fell into a daze and fell asleep.

Then, Jiang Yihua seemingly heard rhythmic drumbeats from afar, and he went into the direction where the sound came from. He arrived at a hill on a river bank. He saw numerous gigantic wooden warships approaching from the distance, the ships linked together by an iron chain. On the ships, rows of soldiers waved their weapons up and down, when, suddenly, the sound of a horn could be heard. A countless number of fire arrows rained down on the warships in the river. The warships caught fire, thick smoke billowing over the river.

They were tightly linked by the chain, with no way to separate. Soon, they were ablaze.

"Clap!" An arrow landed to Jiang Yihua's feet. In fear, he woke up, opened his eyes and found himself lying in bed. It was just a dream about the Battle of Red Cliffs, about the few, weak soldiers of the Sun–Liu Alliance defeating Cao Cao's mighty and imposing army. He intends to tell his teachers and classmates about this Three Kingdoms story of his dreams.

词 语

英 雄 　yīngxióng
　hero; heroic

智 慧 　zhìhuì
　wisdom

xī yǐn 吸 引	attract; draw; fascinate
rén yì 仁 义	benevolence and righteousness
zhí dé 值 得	worth; deserve
hóng dà 宏 大	grand; great
yǐ ruòshèng qiáng 以 弱 胜 强	using the weak to defeat the strong; to win from a position of weakness
yī xí zhī dì 一 席 之 地	a proper/an acknowledged place (or standing)

yǐng xiǎng 影 响	influence; effect; affect
zhōng chéng 忠 诚	loyal; faithful
zhàn shèng 战 胜	defeat; triumph over; vanquish
zhèn hàn rén xīn 震 撼 人 心	stirring; thrilling
fàn lì 范 例	example; model
lè bù sī shǔ 乐 不 思 蜀	so happy as to forget home and duty; indulge in pleasures

jǔ yī fǎn sān 举 一 反 三	raise one and infer three; de-duce many things from one case	fú xiàn 浮 现	appear before one's eyes; come back (to mind); appear; emerge
tiě liàn 铁 链	iron chain	huī dòng 挥 动	brandish; wave
hào jiǎo 号 角	horn	nóng yān gǔn gǔn 浓 烟 滚 滚	thick smoke billowing

专 有 名 词

1. 赤壁 / Chì Bì /
The Battle of Red Cliffs; The Battle of Chibi; decisive battle fought at the end of the Han Dynasty; Sun Quan and Liu Bei were allied against Cao Cao, who commanded 50,000 men and 800,000 men respectively

2. 三国演义 / Sānguó Yǎnyì /
Romance of the Three Kingdoms; 14th century novel attributed to Luo Guanzhong; part historical, part legend, part mythical

3. 诸葛亮 / Zhūgě Liàng /
Zhuge Liang (181-234); politician, military strategist, writer, engineer and inventor; served as Imperial Chancellor and regent of the state of Shu Han

4. 微信 / wēi xìn / WeChat

语言点

1. 在……中占有一席之地
2. 以……胜……（以弱胜强）

思考

1. 除了"赤壁之战"，你还知道三国时期的著名战役吗？

2. 你还知道哪些跟三国文化有关系的书籍、电影、游戏什么的？

3. 你觉得赤壁之战孙刘联盟战胜曹操的主要原因有哪些？假设当时蜀国和吴国没有联盟，你觉得三国的历史会怎样发展？

4. 假如你是曹操，你会怎样来打赤壁之战？怎样去避免曹操犯下的错误？

第二课 【三国时代】
Lesson 2 【The Three Kingdoms Era】

① 特 殊　tèshū
② 朝 代　cháodài
③ 统 一　tǒngyī
④ 分 裂　fēnliè

江一华：

老师，昨天我做了一个噩梦，梦到了三国时期的赤壁之战。

老 师：

那个时候战争不断，老百姓的生活也不稳定，吃不饱、穿不暖，生活非常贫苦。

马 兰：

老师，您可以详细讲讲吗？

老 师：

好。三国这段历史比较特殊，三国以前和以后的朝代都是统一的，到了三国，变成分裂的了，就像一块完整的蛋糕被分成了几份。

林 川：

那当时这块"蛋糕"被分成了三份吗？所以这段特殊的时期就是三国时期，对吧？

老 师：

可以这样理解。那三份"蛋糕"里有成都的一份，成都就是三国时期蜀国的都城，当时叫"益州"。

文小西：

哦，怪不得，成都有一条路的名字叫"益州大道"。

马 兰：

老师，三个国家都有了"蛋糕"以后，应该就不会有战争了吧。

老 师：

可是谁愿意只吃自己的那份"蛋糕"呢？三个国家都梦想着再一次统一中国，成为霸主。所以那段时期战争不断。

文小西：

战争让老百姓失去了亲人和家庭，他们当时的日子是最苦的吧。

老 师：

是啊，所以，有人说三国这个时代是一个痛苦的时代。

⑤都 城　　dūchéng
⑥益 州　　Yìzhōu
⑦益州大道　Yìzhōu Dàdào
⑧霸 主　　bàzhǔ

① 天下大事分久必合，
　　合久必分
　　Tiānxià dàshì fēn jiǔ bì hé,
　　hé jiǔ bì fēn
② 秦始皇　　Qín Shǐhuáng
③ 秦　朝　　Qíncháo
④ 汉　朝　　Hàncháo
⑤ 东　汉　　Dōnghàn
⑥ 军　阀　　jūnfá
⑦ 势　力　　shìlì
⑧ 体　验　　tǐyàn
⑨ 遗　留　　yíliú
⑩ 衣冠庙　　Yīguān Miào
⑪ 洗面桥　　Xǐmiàn Qiáo
⑫ 武侯祠　　Wǔhóu Cí

（小阅读）
　　中国有句古话说：天下大事分久必合，合久必分。秦始皇统一中国，秦朝、汉朝国家统一，到了东汉末年，军阀势力越来越大，他们各自占领一些地方，形成了魏、蜀、吴三个国家，简称"三国"（220—280 年）。三国时期，蜀国的国都就是现在的成都。成都与三国这段历史有着密切的联系。如果你想体验三国时期的蜀国文化，不妨租一辆"小黄车"，在成都市区内找一找遗留下来的蜀国古迹，如衣冠庙、洗面桥、武侯祠等，感受一下蜀国的历史与文化。

Jiang Yihua: I had a nightmare yesterday. I dreamt about the Three Kingdom's Battle of Red Cliffs.

Teacher: Back then, there were constant wars. People led lives of uncertainty and neither had sufficient food nor clothing. They were badly off.

Ma Lan: Could you go into detail?

Teacher: All right. The Three Kingdoms period is bit of a special part of history. The dynasties before and afterwards ruled over one united country. During the Three Kingdoms, the country became divided, just like a whole cake being divided into several pieces.

Lin Chuan: Back then, was this "cake" divided into three pieces? This is why this special period is the Three Kingdoms era, right?

Teacher: Yes, you can see it this way. One of these three pieces of "cake" was Chengdu. Chengdu was the capital of Shu during the Three Kingdoms period and called "Yizhou".

Wen Xiaoxi: Ah, no wonder there's a street called "Yizhou Avenue" in Chengdu.

Ma Lan: After these three countries having had their "cake", there was no more war then, I suppose.

Teacher: But who only wants to enjoy their share of the "cake"? All three countries dreamt of uniting China once again and becoming its overlord. That is why there was constant war during that time.

Wen Xiaoxi: War makes people lose their loved ones and their families. It was they who endured the most suffering at that time.

Teacher: Absolutely, so some say that the Three Kingdoms era was an era of pain and suffering.

Small reading exercise:
There is an old saying in China: What is long divided, must unite; what is long united, must divide. Qin Shi Huang unified China. During the Qin and Han Dynasties, the country was one. By the end of the Eastern Han Dynasty, the warlords were getting increasingly powerful. Each of them occupied several places and formed three countries, namely "Wei", "Shu" and "Wu". Together, they were called the Three Kingdoms (220-280). During the Three Kingdoms era, Shu was today's Chengdu. Chengdu and the history of the Three Kingdoms are closely interconnected. If you want to experience Shu culture, there is no harm in renting a "yellow bicycle" (by ofo) and go look for the historic sites left over by Shu in the Chengdu city area, such as Yiguan Temple, Ximian Bridge and Wuhou Temple, immersing yourself in the history and culture of Shu.

词语

 fēnliè
split; divide; break up

 dūchéng
capital (of a country)

tè shū 特 殊	special; exceptional		bà zhǔ 霸 主	overlord; hegemon
tǒng yī 统 一	unify; unite		dū chéng 都 城	capital (of a country)
jūn fá 军 阀	warlord		shì lì 势 力	force; power; influence
tǐ yàn 体 验	experience for oneself		yí liú 遗 留	leave over; hand down

专有名词

1. 益州   / Yìzhōu / Yizhou

2. 益州大道 / Yìzhōu Dàdào/ Yizhou Avenue

3. 秦朝   / Qíncháo / Qin Dynasty (226BC-206 BC)

4. 衣冠庙 / Yīguān Miào / Yiguan Temple

5. 汉朝 / Hàncháo / Han Dynasty (206 BC-220 AD)

6. 东汉 / Dōnghàn / Eastern Han Dynasty (25-220 AD)

7. 洗面桥 / Xǐmiàn Qiáo / Ximian Bridge

8. 武侯祠 / Wǔhóu Cí / Wuhou Temple; Memorial Temple of Marquis Wu

9. 秦始皇 / Qín Shǐhuáng / Qin Shi Huang (259BC-210BC); lit: "First Emperor of Qin" ; founder of Qin Dynasty and the first emperor of a unified China

俗 语

Tiān xià dà shì fēn jiǔ bì hé, 天 下 大 事 分 久 必 合， hé jiǔ bì fēn 合 久 必 分	What is long divided, must unite; what is long united, must divide.

语 言 点

不妨

思 考

1. 三国时期蜀国的都城在哪儿?

2. 你能简单说一说三国时期的时代背景吗?

3. 请问在你的国家或者世界上别的国家有没有与三国时期很相似的时期? 你可以比较一下有什么相同和不同的地方吗?

第三课【三国之蜀国英雄】
Lesson 3【Heroes of Shu of the Three Kingdoms】

林川：

战争时代，老百姓们这么苦，谁能来帮助他们改变痛苦的生活呢？

老师：

中国人常说"乱世出英雄"，在这样一个特殊时期，出现了大家熟悉的英雄人物，比如刘备、诸葛亮、关羽、张飞等。

文小西：

哦，我知道这些英雄。我们在锦里街的小店里见过这些人物的工艺品，做得非常精美，我很喜欢，真想买几个回家。

江一华：

但是我发现每个人物脸上的颜色都不一样，比如关羽的脸是红色的，曹操的脸又那么白。

① 乱世出英雄 Luànshì chū yīngxióng
② 刘备 Liúbèi
③ 关羽 Guānyǔ
④ 张飞 Zhāngfēi
⑤ 锦里 Jǐnlǐ
⑥ 精美 jīngměi

⑦ 曹 操　Cáocāo
⑧ 川 剧　Chuānjù
⑨ 手 法　shǒufǎ
⑩ 象 征　xiàngzhēng
⑪ 正 直　zhèngzhí
⑫ 阴 险　yīnxiǎn
⑬ 一个唱红脸，一个唱白脸
　　Yígè chàng hóngliǎn，
　　yígè chàng báiliǎn
⑭ 扮 演　bànyǎn
⑮ 严 厉　yánlì
⑯ 温 和　wēnhé
⑰ 学 问　xuéwèn

老师：
这是川剧的一种艺术表现手法，红脸象征正直的好人，白脸象征阴险的坏人。中文有一句俗语——"一个唱红脸，一个唱白脸"，说的就是这个意思。

马兰：
就是一个人扮演好人，另一个人扮演坏人吗？

老师：
举个例子，比如中国的父母在教育小孩的时候，父母常扮演不同的角色。爸爸可能是那个很严厉的人，妈妈可能是那个温和的人，那么可以说他们俩是"一个唱红脸，一个唱白脸"。

林川：
哦，原来还有这么多学问。

Lin Chuan: During these years of war, the common people suffered so much; who would help them make their lives better?

Teacher: The Chinese often say, "Turbulent times call for great heroes." In this special period, the heroes you all are familiar with emerged, for example, Liu Bei, Zhuge Liang, Guan Yu, Zhang Fei and so on.

Wen Xiaoxi: Ah, I know these heroes! We saw handicraft related to them in the shops in Jinli Street. They were elegantly made, and they stroke my fancy. I really wanted to buy some and take them home.

Jiang Yihua: I found that each of these characters' face colors are different. Guan Yu's face, for example, is red, and Cao Cao's is really white.

Teacher: This is a kind of artistic expression of Sichuan opera. The red face symbolizes integrity, while the white face is a symbol of sinister, bad people. There is a common saying in Chinese, "One wears the red mask; the other the white mask", which means just that.

Ma Lan: Does that mean that one person plays the role of the hero, while the other one plays the role of the villain?

Teacher: For example, Chinese parents play different roles in the education of their children. The father may be the strict one, while the mother may be the gentle one. You may then say, "One wears the red mask, the other the white mask."

Lin Chuan: Oh, who would have thought there's so much to learn!

词 语

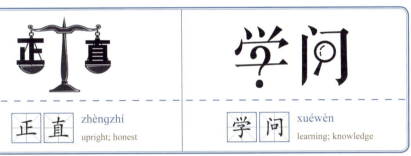

正 直	zhèngzhí upright; honest	学 问	xuéwèn learning; knowledge

shú xī 熟 悉	know sth. or sb. well; be familiar with	jīng měi 精 美	exquisite; elegant; beautiful
shǒu fǎ 手 法	skill; technique	xiàng zhēng 象 征	symbol; symbolize
yīn xiǎn 阴 险	sinister; insidious; treacherous	yán lì 严 厉	stern; strict
wēn hé 温 和	gentle; mild	bàn yǎn 扮 演	play the part of; act

专 有 名 词

1. 锦里 / Jǐnlǐ / Jinli

2. 川剧 / Chuānjù / Sichuan Opera

3. 刘备 / Liú Bèi / Liu Bei (161-223); founder and first ruler of Shu Han

4. 关 羽　/ Guān Yǔ / Guan Yu (160-220); general serving under Liu Bei

5. 张 飞　/ Zhāng Fēi / Zhang Fei (约 160-221); general serving under Liu Bei

6. 曹 操　/ Cáo Cāo / Cao Cao (155-220); penultimate Chancellor of the Eastern Han Dynasty, who laid the foundations for the state of Cao Wei

俗 语

Luàn shì chū yīng xióng 乱 世 出 英 雄	Turbulent times call for great heroes.
Yí gè chàng hóng liǎn, 一 个 唱 红 脸, Yí gè chàng bái liǎn 一 个 唱 白 脸	One coaxes, the other coerces; play good cop bad cop.

思 考

1. 你比较喜欢三国的哪一位英雄人物？为什么？

2. 川剧人物脸谱的颜色表示什么意思？

3. 在这一课我们了解了中国戏剧用不同颜色的脸谱来表现不同的人物性格，请问你知不知道戏剧表演中还有什么样的表现人物性格的方法？

第四课 【刘备与"桃园三结义"】
Lesson 4 【Liu Bei and the "Oath of the Peach Garden"】

① 运气　yùnqì
② 一个好汉三个帮
　　Yígè hǎohàn sāngè bāng
③ 厚道　hòu dao
④ 仗义　zhàngyì
⑤ 爱惜　àixī
⑥ 结拜　jiébài

江一华：

老师，我小时候听爷爷讲过小说《三国演义》，刘备的运气可真好啊，有那么多好朋友帮助他。

老师：

是啊，中国人常说："一个好汉三个帮。"刘备做人厚道，对兄弟们很仗义；他温和善良，也很爱惜人才。所以很多人都愿意帮助他。

林川：

我和江一华也是好朋友呢，我们也总是互相帮忙。每次我遇到了汉语问题，都会先问问一华，他总是耐心地帮我。

文小西：

哈哈，那你们也结拜成兄弟吧。

老 师：
你们也应该像桃园三位英雄一样，做志同道合的朋友，有一样的梦想——学好汉语。只要互相帮助，一起努力，梦想一定能实现。

江一华：
林川，我们要一起加油啦！

马 兰：
老师，怎么诸葛亮没有跟他们结拜成兄弟呢？

老 师：
那个时候刘备还没遇到诸葛亮，也还没有刘备"三顾茅庐"请诸葛亮帮忙的故事。

⑦ 志同道合　zhìtóng-dàohé
⑧ 君 主　jūnzhǔ
⑨ 善 于　shànyú
⑩ 高 明　gāomíng
⑫ 杰 出　jiéchū
⑬ 一见如故　yíjiàn-rúgù
⑭ 志趣相投　zhìqù-xiāngtóu
⑮ 于 是　yúshì
⑯ 出生入死　chūshēng-rùsǐ
⑰ 争 夺　zhēngduó
⑱ 功不可没　gōngbùkěmò

（小阅读）

蜀国的君王刘备善于识人用人，是一个高明的领导。他从小就有远大的理想，结识了一批杰出的朋友。小说《三国演义》中写到，刘备遇到关羽和张飞，他们三人一见如故，志趣相投，于是在桃园结拜为兄弟，刘备是大哥，关羽是二哥，张飞是三弟。从此，关羽与张飞一直陪伴刘备，为他出生入死，帮助他争夺天下。这个故事就叫作"桃园三结义"。刘备后来能建立蜀国，他的这些好兄弟们功不可没。

Jiang Yihua: When I was a kid, I listened to my grandfather talk about the *Romance of the Three Kingdoms*. Liu Bei was a lucky man that he had so many friends helping him out.

Teacher: True. The Chinese often say, "An able man needs the help of three other people." Liu Bei was honest and kind, and loyal towards his brothers. He was a kind and loving man who also valued talent, so many people were eager to help him.

Lin Chuan: I am also good friends with Jiang Yihua; we always help each other. Every time I come across a problem in Chinese, I'll ask Yihua first. He is always patient with me.

Wen Xiaoxi: (Laughing) Then you two are also sworn brothers now.

Teacher: I suppose you're like the three heroes in the peach garden, like-minded friends who share the same dream: learn Chinese well. As long as you help each other and work together, you will definitely be able to make your dream come true.

Jiang Yihua: Lin Chuan, we'll give it our best!

Ma Lan: How come Zhuge Liang did not become sworn brothers with them?

Teacher: At that point in time, Liu Bei hadn't met Zhuge Liang yet. Liu Bei also hadn't paid his three humble visits to a thatched cottage and asked Zhuge Liang for help.

Small reading exercise:
Liu Bei, ruler of Shu, was a clever leader who knew how to identify and use talented people. From very early on, he had lofty ideals and became friends with a group of outstanding people. As is described in *Romance of the Three Kingdoms*, Liu Bei met Guan Yu and Zhang Fei, and the three of them were like old friends from the start, sharing similar aspirations and interests. This is why they swore to be brothers in the Peach Garden: Liu Bei was the eldest, Guan Yu was the second and Zhang Fei the third brother. Since then, Guan Yu and Zhang Fei always accompanied Liu Bei and went for him through fire and water in the fight for China. This story is called "The Oath of the Peach Garden". Later, Liu Bei managed to found the state of Shu and his brothers' contributions did not go unnoticed.

词语

 àixī
value highly; treasure

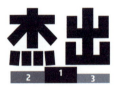

 jiéchū
outstanding; remarkable; prominent

yùn qì 运 气	fortune; luck
zhàng yì 仗 义	loyal (to one's friends); generous and ready to offer help
jié bài 结 拜	become sworn brothers or sisters
shàn yú 善 于	be good at; be adept in
jié shí 结 识	get acquainted with sb; get to know
zhì qù xiāng tóu 志 趣 相 投	kindred spirits; have similar aspiration and interests

hòu dao 厚 道	honest and kind
jūn zhǔ 君 主	monarch; sovereign
zhì tóng dào hé 志 同 道 合	cherish the same ideals and follow the same path; have a common goal; like-minded
gāo míng 高 明	brilliant; wise
yí jiàn rú gù 一 见 如 故	feel like old friends at the first meeting; hit it off well right from the start; like old friends from the start
yú shì 于 是	accordingly; so; hence; then; thereupon; as a result

chū shēng 出 生 rù sǐ 入 死	from the cradle to the grave; go through fire and water; willing to risk life and limb; brave untold dangers	gōng bù kě mò 功 不 可 没	one's contributions cannot go unnoticed
		zhēng duó 争 夺	fight for; contend for

俗 语

Yí gè hǎo hàn sān gè bāng 一 个 好 汉 三 个 帮	An able man needs the help of three other people; two heads are better than one

思 考

你能简单介绍一下"桃园三结义"的故事吗？

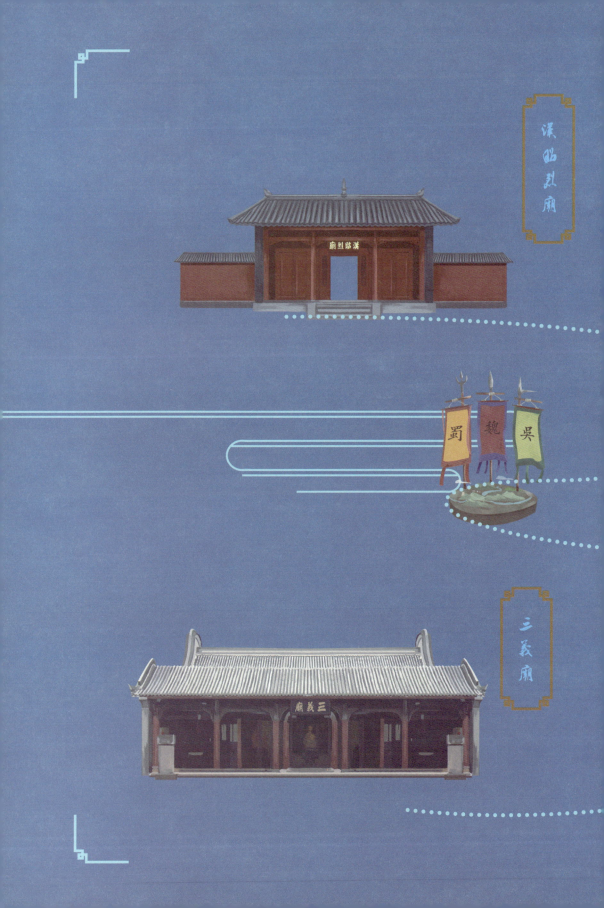

汉昭烈庙

蜀 魏 吴

三义庙

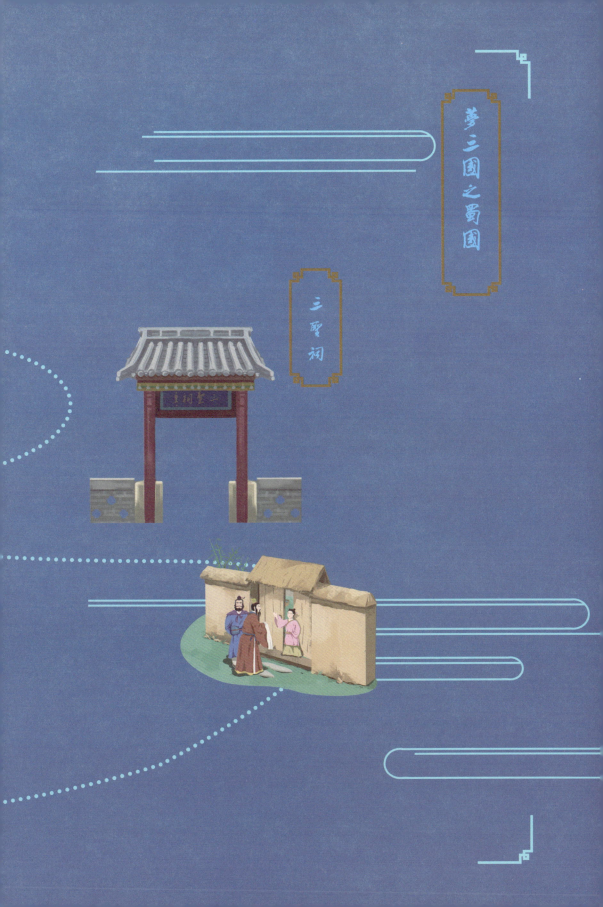

夢三國之蜀國

三聖祠

第五课 【刘备与"三顾茅庐"】

Lesson 5 【 Liu Bei and His "Three Humble Visits to a Thatched Cottage" 】

马兰：

老师，刘备是怎么认识诸葛亮的呢？那时候不可能自己在网上投简历应聘吧。

① 名 气　míngqì
② 推 荐　tuījiàn
③ 采 纳　cǎinà
④ 主 动　zhǔdòng

江一华：

当时诸葛亮小有名气，有人向刘备推荐了诸葛亮，是吧？

老师：

是的。刘备采纳了朋友的建议，主动去诸葛亮的家请诸葛亮帮他，这就是著名的"三顾茅庐"的故事。

林川：

"三顾茅庐"？刘备去了三次诸葛亮的家才请到他吗？

老师：

对呀。优秀的人才可不是那么容易就得到的。刘备第三次去诸葛亮的家时，诸葛亮才决定跟他见面。

⑤耐 心　　nàixīn
⑥具 备　　jùbèi
⑦实 力　　shílì
⑧放 弃　　fàngqì
⑨坚持不懈　jiānchí-búxiè

文小西：
刘备可真有耐心啊。

马 兰：
这也能看出来刘备非常看重人才、珍惜人才。

林 川：
是啊，要想获得成功，除了自己要具备实力，手下的员工也得个个优秀啊。

老 师：
对，你们说得很好！"三顾茅庐"的故事也告诉我们一个道理：遇到困难，只要坚持不放弃，就一定可以成功。

文小西：
我同意。学习汉语也是一样的，虽然学习的过程比较辛苦，但是只要我们坚持不懈，就一定能学好。

⑩技 巧　　jìqiǎo
⑪才华出众　cáihuá-chūzhòng
⑫欲擒故纵　yùqín gùzòng
⑬来之不易　láizhī búyì
⑭考 验　　kǎoyàn
⑮名不虚传　míngbù xūchuán

江一华：

老师，我觉得诸葛亮非常有智慧，让刘备来了三次才见面，这是不是他的"求职"技巧呀？

老 师：

你说的也有道理。当时的刘备急需一个才华出众的人，诸葛亮用"欲擒故纵"的方式的确可以吸引刘备，这就像一顿美食，等待的时间越长，你越觉得美味。同样刘备也会认为得到诸葛亮的帮助来之不易，会更加珍惜。

马 兰：

对呀，我觉得诸葛亮也可能用这样的方法来考验刘备是不是真心想请他帮忙。

江一华：

小时候我就听爷爷说过诸葛亮非常聪明，真是名不虚传。对了，我以前还放过"孔明灯"，听说也跟诸葛亮有关系？

老 师：

孔明灯又叫"天灯"，是诸葛亮发明的，因为诸葛亮字"孔明"，所以叫"孔明灯"。你们知道中国人为什么放"孔明灯"吗？

⑯照 明　zhàomíng
⑰孔明灯　Kǒngmíng Dēng
⑱祈 福　qífú
⑲谦 虚　qiānxū
⑳手 下　shǒuxià

林川：
　　我觉得是因为古时候没有电，所以人们用这种灯照明。

老师：
　　当然不是啦，人们放"孔明灯"是为了祈福。

林川：
　　哦，原来是这样。下次我们也去试一试。

（小阅读）
　　当年，刘备听说诸葛亮特别有能力，就带着关羽和张飞去拜访。诸葛亮为了弄清楚刘备到底是不是一个谦虚的好领导，就在刘备第一次和第二次光顾时都说自己出去了，没有跟刘备见面。刘备跟关羽、张飞第三次来到诸葛亮家时，诸葛亮正在睡午觉，刘备一直站在门外等他醒来。最后，诸葛亮终于被刘备感动了，答应帮助他。这就是著名的"三顾茅庐"的故事。后来诸葛亮也成了刘备的手下，帮助刘备建立了蜀国。

Ma Lan: How did Liu Bei come to know Zhuge Liang? Back then you couldn't just put your CV on the Internet and apply.

Jiang Yihua: At that time Zhuge Liang already made a name for himself. I suppose somebody recommended Zhuge Liang to Liu Bei.

Teacher: Correct. Liu Bei accepted a friend's suggestion to take the initiative in going to Zhuge Liang's home and asking him for help. This is the story of his "three humble visits to a thatched cottage".

Lin Chuan: "Three humble visits to a thatched cottage"? Liu Bei went to Zhuge Liang's home to ask for his help?

Teacher: Yes! Outstanding people are not easy to get. Only when Liu Bei went to Zhuge Liang's home for the third time did Zhuge Liang agree to meet with him.

Wen Xiaoxi: Liu Bei's really patient!

Ma Lan: You can also see that Liu Bei attaches great importance and value to talented people.

Lin Chuan: Absolutely! If you want to be successful, not only do you have to be capable yourself, every member of your "staff" also needs to be outstanding.

Teacher: Right, well said! The story of "three humble visits to a thatched cottage"also tells us a moral: if you face difficulties, whatever you do, don't give up, and you will succeed.

Wen Xiaoxi: I agree. It's the same with studying Chinese. Although the process is quite arduous, as long as we persevere, we will get good results.

Jiang Yihua: I think Zhuge Liang is incredibly wise; he let Liu Bei come three times before meeting with him, couldn't that be called a "job searching technique"of his?

Teacher: You could put it that way. At that time, Liu Bei was in urgent need of outstanding and talented people. Zhuge Liang adopted the "in order to capture, one must let loose" method to draw Liu Bei to him. You may compare this to a serving of delicious food, which becomes even more tasty the longer you have to wait. The same applies to Liu Bei who may have thought Zhuge Liang's help isn't easy to come by, so he would cherish it even more.

Ma Lan: Right, I think Zhuge Liang may also have used this method to test Liu Bei whether he really wanted to ask Zhuge Liang for help.

Jiang Yihua: When I was a child, I heard my grandfather say that Zhuge Liang was very clever. He really lives up to his reputation. By the way, I launched a "Kongming lantern" once. I heard it is also connected with Zhuge Liang.

Teacher: Kongming lanterns are also called "sky lanterns" and were invented by Zhuge Liang. His courtesy name was "Kongming", so the lanterns were named "Kongming lantern". Do you know why the Chinese launch Kongming lanterns?

Lin Chuan: I think it's because they didn't have electricity in the ancient times, so they used the lanterns for lighting.

Teacher: Not really. They launch "Kongming lanterns" to pray for blessings.

Lin Chuan: Oh, so that's why! Next time we'll also give it a try!

Small reading exercise:
Back then, Liu Bei heard that Zhuge Liang was a particularly able man, and paid him a visit with Guan Yu and Zhang Fei in tow. In order to find out whether Liu Bei was a modest and good leader or not, he told Liu Bei at his first and second visit that Zhuge Liang went out and did not meet with Liu Bei. When Liu Bei with Guan Yu and Zhang Fei went to Zhuge Liang's home for the third time, the latter was taking a nap, and Liu Bei stood outside and waited for Zhuge Liang to wake up. Finally, he was touched by Liu Bei's dedication and agreed to help him. This is the famous story of the "three humble visits to a thatched cottage". Later, Zhuge Liang became Liu Bei's subordinate, and helped him found Shu.

词语

放弃	祈福

放弃	fàngqì abandon; give up	祈福	qífú pray for good fortune

míng qì 名 气	reputation; fame
cǎi nà 采 纳	accept (opini- ons, suggestions, requests, etc.); follow (advice)
nài xīn 耐 心	patient
shí lì 实 力	strength
jì qiǎo 技 巧	skill; technique
lái zhī bú yì 来 之 不 易	not easily come by; hard-earned

tuī jiàn 推 荐	recommend
zhǔ dòng 主 动	take the iniative; do sth. of one's own accord; (pro-)active
jù bèi 具 备	possess; have
jiān chí bú xiè 坚 持 不 懈	unremitting; persistent
cái huá chū zhòng 才 华 出 众	outstanding and talented
kǎo yàn 考 验	test

míng bù xū chuán 名 不 虚 传	have a well-deserved reputation; live up to one's reputation
qiān xū 谦 虚	modest

zhào míng 照 明	illuminate; light up
shǒu xià 手 下	subordinate

yù qín gù zòng 欲 擒 故 纵	in order to capture, one must let loose; loosen the reins only to grasp them better; leave sb. at large the better to apprehend him; give sb. rope enough to hang himself

专 有 名 词

孔明灯　/Kǒngmíng Dēng / Kongming lantern; Chinese lantern; sky lantern (a small hot air balloon made of paper, with an opening at the bottom where a small fire is suspended)

语 言 点

到底

思 考

1. 为什么刘备来了三次，诸葛亮才愿意跟他见面？

2. 请你简单介绍一下"三顾茅庐"的故事。

3. 请你说一说"三顾茅庐"的故事对你有什么样的启发。

4. 现在中国人为什么放"孔明灯"呢？

第六课 【诸葛亮与"空城计"】
Lesson 6 【Zhuge Liang and the "Empty Fort Strategy"】

大 萌：

三国故事中有很多历史故事都体现了诸葛亮的聪明才智。

① 攻　　gōng
② 抵 抗　dǐkàng
③ 危 机　wēijī
④ 冷 静　lěngjìng
⑤ 埋 伏　máifú
⑥ 撤 退　chètuì
⑦ 计 策　jìcè

江 一华：

有哪些故事呢？

老 师：

比如说"空城计"。据说当时敌人来攻城的时候，蜀国大部分年轻的士兵们都出城了，城里只剩下很少的士兵，还有一些老人、妇女和孩子，根本不能抵抗强大的敌人。

文 小西：

没有足够多的士兵可怎么办啊？

老 师：

在危急的情况下，诸葛亮冷静地坐在城楼上弹琴，并且让士兵们打开城门，敌军看诸葛亮那么冷静，担心里面有埋伏，不敢进城，很快撤退了。诸葛亮用这个计策成功地吓走了敌人。

⑧胆 量　　dǎnliàng

⑨三个臭皮匠，赛过诸葛亮

　　Sāngè chòupíjiàng,

　　sàiguò Zhūgě Liàng

⑩发 挥　　fāhuī

⑪集 体　　jítǐ

⑫毕 竟　　bìjìng

⑬出谋划策　chūmóu huàcè

⑭克 服　　kèfú

⑮地地道道　dìdì dàodào

文小西：

哇！诸葛亮不仅有智慧而且有胆量，我好崇拜他。

老师：

俗话说："三个臭皮匠，赛过诸葛亮。"只要发挥集体的智慧，普通人也能做出了不起的事情。所以不用羡慕诸葛明的聪明，毕竟像他那样的人才太少了。

马兰：

遇到问题的时候只要大家团结合作，一起出谋划策，什么困难都能克服。

文小西：

听老师讲完"空城计"，我的肚子也开始唱"空城计"了，我们一起想想中午吃什么吧。

马兰：

你真是一个地地道道的"吃货"，我看你的钱包也快唱"空城计"了吧。

（小阅读）

诸葛亮辅佐刘备打天下，帮助刘备建立了蜀汉政权，并展现出了治理国家的杰出才能。诸葛亮重视蜀地农业和都江堰水利工程的发展，把蜀国治理得井井有条，他让蜀国老百姓过上了丰衣足食的生活，受到蜀国老百姓的爱戴和崇拜，历史学家评价他为优秀的政治家。不过在三国的文学作品和民间传说中，诸葛亮被看作一个天才，神机妙算，是一个被神化了的人物，具有半人半神的超人形象。无论是历史学家对诸葛亮的评价，还是文学作品和民间传说中的形象，诸葛亮都是一位了不起的英雄。

① 辅 佐　　fǔzuǒ
② 治 理　　zhìlǐ
③ 都江堰　　Dūjiāngyàn
④ 水 利　　shuǐlì
⑤ 工 程　　gōngchéng
⑥ 井井有条　jǐngjǐng yǒutiáo
⑦ 丰衣足食　fēngyī-zúshí
⑧ 爱 戴　　àidài
⑨ 政治家　　zhèngzhìjiā
⑩ 神机妙算　shénjī miàosuàn

Da Meng: Among the Three Kingdoms stories are many historical ones that show Zhuge Liang's ingenuity.

Jiang Yihua: What stories?

Teacher: The "Empty Fort Strategy", for example. It is said that when enemy forces came to attack the city, most of the young soldiers of Shu were out of town, leaving only a small number of soldiers, some elderly, women and children behind, who were completely unable to resist the powerful enemy.

Wen Xiaoxi: If they didn't have enough soldiers, what was their plan?

Teacher: Amidst the crisis, Zhuge Liang calmly sat in the gate tower and played the Guqin. He ordered the soldiers to open the gates. When the enemy saw the calm Zhuge Liang, they worried that an ambush lied in wait for them. They weren't brave enough to enter the fort and quickly retreated. Zhuge Liang successfully scared away the enemy with his stratagem.

Wen Xiaoxi: Wow! Zhuge Liang is not only wise, but daring, too! I adore him!

Teacher: As the saying goes, "Three cobblers with their wits combined surpass Zhuge Liang the master mind." As long as they collectively use their wisdom, ordinary people can also deliver incredible results. So, don't envy Zhuge Liang for his wisdom, because there are few like him.

Ma Lan: We can surmount any difficulties we encounter as long as we stand and plan together.

Wen Xiaoxi: After listening to our teacher talking about the "Empty Fort Strategy", my tummy is also starting to rumble to the tune of an empty fort. Let's discuss what we'll have for lunch.

Ma Lan: You are an out and out foodie. Your wallet is also singing to the tune of an empty fort, I take it.

Small reading exercise:
Zhuge Liang assisted Liu Bei in his conquest, helped him found the state of Shu Han, and demonstrated outstanding ability to govern the country. Zhuge Liang attached great importance to Shu's agricultural development and the Dujiangyan Irrigation Project, and organized Shu in an orderly manner. He allowed the people in Shu to live a life of plenty and was loved and worshipped by them. Historians consider him an excellent politician. In the literary works and folklore about the Three Kingdoms, Zhuge Liang is seen as a genius who was supremely clever in his schemes. He was a deified figure with a half human-half superhuman image. Be it historians' assessments or the image described in literary works and folklore, Zhuge Liang was a remarkable hero.

词语

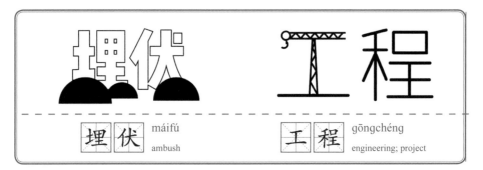

埋 伏	máifú
	ambush

工 程	gōngchéng
	engineering; project

gōng 攻	attack
wēi jí 危 急	critical
chè tuì 撤 退	withdraw; pull out
dǎn liàng 胆 量	courage; guts
jí tǐ 集 体	collective
chū móu huà cè 出 谋 划 策	put forward plans and ideas; give counsel; mastermind

dǐ kàng 抵 抗	resist; stand up to
lěng jìng 冷 静	calm
jì cè 计 策	stratagem; plan; ploy
fā huī 发 挥	display; exhibit; express; bring out implicit or innate qualities
bì jìng 毕 竟	after all
kè fú 克 服	surmount; overcome

dì dì dào dào 地 地 道 道	out and out; outright; one hundred percent; to the core
zhì lǐ 治 理	administer; govern
jǐng jǐng yǒu tiáo 井 井 有 条	in perfect order; shipshape; methodical
ài dài 爱 戴	love and esteem; adore

fǔ zuǒ 辅 佐	assist (a ruler) (in governing a country)
shuǐ lì 水 利	irrigation works; water conservancy project
fēng yī zú shí 丰 衣 足 食	have ample food and clothing; be well-fed and well-clothed; live a life of plenty
zhèng zhì jiā 政 治 家	politician

shén jī miào suàn 神 机 妙 算	divine strategy and wonderful planning; clever scheme; supremely clever in his schemes; wonderful foresight

专 有 名 词

都江堰 / Dūjiāngyàn / Dujiangyan; ancient irrigation system in Dujiangyan City,
Sichuan, in the west part of the Chengdu Plain

俗 语

sān gè chòu pí jiàng, 三 个 皮 神 匠, sài guò Zhū gě Liàng 赛 过 诸 葛 亮	three cobblers with their wits combined surpass Zhuge Liang the master mind; the wisdom of the masses exceeds that of the wisest individual; two heads are better than one

思 考

1. 你认为诸葛亮是一位什么样的人？

2. 你还知道关于诸葛亮智慧的故事吗？

3. 如果你是攻城的人，你有什么样的方法可以破解诸葛亮的空城计？

第七课 【关羽和张飞】
Lesson 7 【Guan Yu and Zhang Fei】

① 华 人　huárén
② 祭 拜　jìbài
③ 关公庙　Guāngōng Miào
④ 勇 猛　yǒngměng
⑤ 财神爷　cáishényé
⑥ 塑 像　sùxiàng
⑦ 称 呼　chēnghu
⑧ 保 佑　bǎoyòu
⑨ 兴 隆　xīnglóng
⑩ 财源广进　cáiyuán guǎngjìn
⑪ 入乡随俗　rùxiāng-suísú
⑫ 发 财　fācái

江一华：
老师，在我们国家，很多华人都特别崇拜关羽，我爷爷就常去关公庙祭拜他。

林 川：
为什么那么多华人喜欢和崇拜关羽呢？

老 师：
因为大家都认为关羽勇猛、忠诚，现在还有很多中国人把关羽当作财神爷，很多商店里都摆放着他的塑像，人们亲切地称呼他"关二爷"，希望他能保佑家人平安，保佑生意兴隆、财源广进。

江一华：
那我也要入乡随俗，下次去关公庙里拜一拜他。

你是想请"关二爷"保佑你发财吧。

⑬卤　　lǔ
⑭犒劳　kàoláo
⑮突出　tūchū
⑯气概　qìgài
⑰鲁莽　lǔmǎng
⑱绣　　xiù

文小西：

　　你们别做发财梦了，下课以后我们去买张飞牛肉吃吧，我还是对美食最感兴趣。

马兰：

　　对了，老师，正想问问你呢，我们在锦里见过卖牛肉的张飞，他真的会做牛肉吗？

老师：

　　当然不是。据说每次打了胜仗，张飞都会用一种卤过的牛肉犒劳将士们，现在的人们把这种牛肉取名为"张飞牛肉"。

文小西：

　　我觉得张飞的样子挺可怕的。

老师：

　　那是现代人根据戏曲里张飞的样子装扮的。黑脸、大眼睛是为了突出张飞的英雄气概，有的小说也把张飞写成性格鲁莽的人，其实张飞是个美男子，而且很细心。

⑲ 张飞穿针 —— 粗中有细
  Zhāng Fēi chuān zhēn ——
  cū zhōng yǒu xì

⑳ 武艺   wǔyì

㉑ 高强   gāoqiáng

㉒ 武圣   Wǔshèng

㉓ 文圣   Wénshèng

㉔ 将军   jiāngjūn

㉕ 坚决   jiānjué

㉖ 千里迢迢   qiānlǐ-tiáotiáo

㉗ 长坂坡   Chángbǎnpō

㉘ 左膀右臂   zuǒbǎng-yòubì

江一华：

对，有句歇后语"张飞穿针——粗中有细"，说的就是张飞的细心。

马兰：

真是人不可貌相！

（小阅读）

刘备有两位好兄弟——关羽和张飞。关羽武艺高强，善于打仗，被后人称为"武圣"，与"文圣"孔子一起，受到人们的崇拜。在各个城市都有为了祭拜关羽修建的关公庙。关羽对刘备非常忠心。他曾经被曹操抓住，曹操想请他当将军。但关羽坚决不答应。曹操送给他美女金钱，他都不要，只接受了曹操送他的一匹宝马。后来他骑着这匹马千里迢迢回到了刘备身边，这就是著名的"千里走单骑"的故事，这个故事一直被中国的戏剧和文学传承，关羽在中国也成了正直忠诚的象征。

张飞也是一位英雄，传说他在长坂坡桥头大吼一声，吓退了曹操百万军队。张飞对刘备也非常忠诚。刘备正是因为有了关羽和张飞这样的左膀右臂，才能从一个普通人成为蜀国的君王。

Jiang Yihua: In our country, ethnic Chinese absolutely adore Guan Yu. My grandpa often goes to a Guan Gong Temple to offer sacrifices.

Lin Chuan: Why do so many Chinese like and worship Guan Yu?

Teacher: Because everybody thinks Guan Yu is brave and loyal. There are still many Chinese who regard Guan Yu as the God of Wealth. Many shops have his statues on display and people affectionately call him"Guan Er Ye" in the hope that he will bless and protect family members, ensure business to be thriving and prosperous and cause money and treasures to be plentiful.

Jiang Yihua: Then I'll also do as the Chinese do and go to a Guan Gong Temple to worship him.

Lin Chuan: You want "Guan Er Ye" to bless you with riches. I take it?

Wen Xiaoxi: Stop dreaming about riches. We'll eat some Zhang Fei beef after class. There's nothing that can beat food!

Ma Lan: By the way, that's also what I wanted to ask you about; we saw a Zhang Fei sell beef in Jinli. Did he really know how to prepare beef?

Teacher: Of course not. Allegedly, every time they were victorious, Zhang Fei would reward his men with stewed beef. Today, this beef is called "Zhang Fei Beef".

Wen Xiaoxi: I think Zhang Fei's appearance is fear-inducing.

Teacher: That's how people dress up as Zhang Fei according to his depiction in Chinese opera. The black face and big eyes serve to bring Zhang Fei's heroic spirit to the fore. Some novels describe Zhang Fei to be reckless; in fact, he was a handsome and attentive man.

Jiang Yihua: As the saying goes, "Zhang Fei threads a needle – a careless person may possess some refined qualities".

Ma Lan: I guess you can't judge a book by its cover!

Small reading exercise:
Liu Bei's two brothers: Guan Yu and Zhang Fei. Guan Yu was skilled in martial arts and excelled in warfare, later known as "the Saint of War", who has been worshipped together with Confucius, "the Saint of Literature". Guan Gong Temples were built in various cities for the worship of Guan Yu. Guan Yu was very loyal towards Liu Bei. He was captured by Cao Cao who wanted him to serve as a general, but Guan Yu vehemently refused. Cao Cao gifted him with beautiful women and money, but Guan Yu refused all of it; he only accepted a precious horse. On this horse's back, he rode all the way to Liu Bei's side, which is how the famous story of "Riding Alone for Thousand Miles" originated. This story was passed on through Chinese opera and literature. Guan Yu became a symbol of integrity and loyalty in China.

Zhang Fei is also a hero, who is said to have roared so imposingly at Changban Slope that he scared away Cao Cao's millions of troops. Zhang Fei was also very loyal to Liu Bei. It was precisely because of Guan Yu and Zhang Fei serving as his right-hand men that Liu Bei was able to turn from a commoner to the ruler of Shu.

词语

| 勇 猛 | yǒngměng
bold and powerful;
brave and fierce |

| 发 财 | fācái

get rich; make a fortune |

huá rén 华 人	(ethnic) Chinese
yǒng měng 勇 猛	bold and powerful; brave and fierce
sù xiàng 塑 像	statue; moulded figure
xīng lóng 兴 隆	prosperous; thriving; flourishing
lǔ 卤	stew in soy sauce and spices
tū chū 突 出	give prominen- ce to; stress; highlight

jì bài 祭 拜	offer sacrifice
cái shén yé 财 神 爷	God of Wealth
chēng hu 称 呼	call; address
cái yuán guǎng jìn 财 源 广 进	treasures fill the home; money and treasures will be plentiful
kào láo 犒 劳	reward with food and drink
qì gài 气 概	loft quality; mettle; spirit

lǔ mǎng 鲁 莽	crude and rash; impulsive; hot-headed; reckless		xiù 绣	embroider
wǔ yì 武 艺	martial art		gāo qiáng 高 强	excel in
jiāng jūn 将 军	general		jiān jué 坚 决	firm; resolute; determined
qiān lǐ tiáo tiáo 千 里 迢 迢	from a thousand li away; from afar; (come) all the way from		zuǒ bǎng yòu bì 左 膀 右 臂	right-hand man; capable assistant

rù xiāng suí sú 入 乡 随 俗	wherever you are, follow local customs; when in Rome, do as the Romans do; do as the natives do

专 有 名 词

1. 关公庙 / Guāngōng Miào / Guan Gong Temple

2. 武圣 / Wǔshèng / Saint of War

3. 文圣 / Wénshèng / Saint of Literature

4. 长坂坡 / Chángbǎnpō / Changban Slope; setting of the Battle of Changban (208 AD)

俗语

| Rén bù kě mào xiàng
人 不 可 貌 相 | you cannot judge a person by his appearance; you cannot judge a book by its cover |

歇后语

| Zhāng Fēi chuān zhēn —— cū zhōng yǒu xì
张 飞 穿 针 —— 粗 中 有 细 | Zhang Fei threads a needle – a careless person may possess some refined qualities; usually careless, but sometimes sharp; crude in most matters, but subtle in some ways |

思考

1. 关羽在中国拥有非常崇高的地位，过去中国很多地方都有关帝庙，很多人特别是商人，都会在自己的店铺中供奉关帝像，请问关羽为什么能在中国获得这么高的地位？这和中国的传统文化价值观有什么关系？

2. 请你说一说关羽和张飞的性格特点。

3. 如果你是刘备，你会跟关羽、张飞结为兄弟吗？为什么？

4. 你还知道哪些关于张飞和关羽的故事？

第八课
Lesson 8

【三国之蜀国遗迹】

【Historical Sites of Shu (of the Three Kingdoms)】

① 着 迷　zháomí
② 见 识　jiànshi
③ 风 采　fēngcǎi
④ 穿 越　chuānyuè
⑤ 佩 服　pèifú
⑥ 亲 眼　qīnyǎn
⑦ 美髯公　měirǎngōng
⑧ 周 仓　Zhōu Cāng
⑨ 青龙偃月刀
　　Qīnglóng Yǎnyuè Dāo

马 兰：

我现在对三国文化已经着迷了，满脑子都是三国的故事和那些英雄人物。

文小西：

对对对，我也有同感。真遗憾我们没有出生在那个时代，不能亲眼见识这些大英雄的风采。要是我们可以穿越回那个时代就好了。

林 川：

如果我能穿越回三国，我一定要去找诸葛亮，他是我最佩服的人，我有好多问题想请教他呢，就算是留在他身边做一个端茶倒水的小童儿我都愿意。

江一华：

如果我能穿越回三国，那我一定要去找关羽，我一定要亲眼看看真正的关羽是不是传说中的大红脸和美髯公，我还要找帮关羽拿刀的周仓，让他把关羽的大刀给我试试，到时候我拿着青龙偃月刀和关羽拍个合影发到朋友圈里，一定会有很多人羡慕我。

⑩不可思议
bùkě sīyì

⑫远在天边近在眼前
Yuǎn zài tiānbiān
jìn zài yǎnqián

老 师：

你们的想象力真是太丰富了。其实你们的穿越梦想并不是天方夜谭，我知道一个地方，能够实现你们的穿越梦。

文小西：

这是真的吗？在哪里？我已经迫不及待要去这个地方了。

老 师：

这个地方远在天边近在眼前，就是成都。

林 川：

老师，您又在跟我们开玩笑吗？成都这么现代化的城市，怎么可能有三国历史的遗迹？

老 师：

成都是中国大城市中保留三国遗迹非常多的一个城市，根据考古、历史和博物馆的专家调查，成都地区一共有 46 处三国遗迹。

江一华：

46 处？这么多？太不可思议了，原来三国历史就在我们的身边啊！

⑬活生生 huóshēngshēng
⑭走 访 zǒufǎng
⑮亲 自 qīnzì

老 师：
对啊，可以说成都就是一座活生生的三国历史
文化遗迹的大展览馆，可能你们走过的一条街
道、进过的一个地铁站、玩过的一个公园、住
过的一个小区，都藏着一个三国的故事和传说。
今天我们就要去走访几个成都最著名的三国历
史遗迹，让你们亲自去触摸、感受和体验三国
文化，去见识那些著名三国人物的风采。

众同学：
哇，太好了，那我们现在就出发吧！

老 师：
好的，三国历史穿越之旅现在开始。

　　三国时期蜀国的首都——四川成都，至今仍保留
着许多三国时期蜀国的历史古迹。走进这些三国古迹，
就好像走进了那段真实的历史，身临其境，感受三国
人物生活过的地方。这些古迹差不多有两千年的历史
了，它静静地向人们讲述着那些引人入胜、波澜壮阔
的故事，拉近人们与历史的距离，让三国不再遥远。
　　如果想了解和体验更多三国之蜀国的历史，那一
定不要错过成都。

一、武侯祠

　　来到成都，有一个有关三国历史的重要遗迹一定要去参观。这个地方就是——武侯祠。如果一个人来到成都没去武侯祠就好像去了北京没去故宫、去了上海没去外滩一样，会留下很多的遗憾。

　　武侯祠是为了纪念诸葛亮而修建的。诸葛亮在成都帮助刘备管理蜀国，为成都百姓做了很多好事，为了纪念他对成都的巨大贡献，人们在他去世后为他修建了一座祠堂。诸葛亮曾经被封为"武乡侯"，去世以后又被追谥为"忠武侯"，所以纪念他的这座祠堂后来就被人们称为"武侯祠"。

　　"武侯祠"的特殊之处还在于它是中国唯一一座君臣合祀的祠堂。"君臣合祀"就是皇帝和大臣被放在同一个祠堂祭祀。在中国古代，皇帝与大臣地位悬殊，大臣是不可能和皇帝放在一起祭祀的。诸葛亮对蜀国贡献巨大，影响深远，因此他能够享受和皇帝刘备放在同一个祠堂这样的待遇。他是中国历史上唯一一位享受这样待遇的人，可见诸葛亮对蜀国的影响之大。

　　武侯祠在成都南边，唐代著名诗人杜甫曾经写诗介绍过武侯祠："丞相祠堂何处寻，锦官城外柏森森。"（《蜀相》）。这两句诗的意思是："纪念诸葛亮的武侯祠在哪里？成都城外长了很多高大的柏树的地方就是。""锦官城"是成都的别名，成都还有个别名——"蓉城"，这是因为古代成都到处都种满了芙蓉花，芙蓉花是成都的市花，所以人们就把成都叫作"蓉城"。

　　武侯祠最早在公元223年开始修建，一千多年来多次遭到破坏又不断重修过几次。现在的祠堂的主体建筑是1672年重建的。它的整个面积有15万平方米，主要包括三个部分：文物区、园林区和锦里。

　　武侯祠最重要的历史遗迹和文物都在文物区。一走进武侯祠的大门，人们首先会看到两边立着六块高

①身临其境	shēnlín qíjìng
②引人入胜	yǐnrén rùshèng
③波澜壮阔	bōlán zhuàngkuò
④遥远	yáoyuǎn
⑤错过	cuòguò
⑥纪念	jìniàn
⑦贡献	gòngxiàn
⑧封	fēng
⑨追谥	zhuīshì
⑩祠堂	cítáng
⑪祭祀	jìsì
⑫悬殊	xuánshū
⑬待遇	dàiyù
⑭杜甫	Dù Fǔ
⑮柏树	bǎishù
⑯锦官城	Jǐnguān Chéng
⑰芙蓉花	fúróng huā
⑱蓉城	Róng Chéng
⑲破坏	pòhuài
⑳主体	zhǔtǐ
㉑清朝	Qīngcháo
㉒文物	wénwù

㉓石 碑　shíbēi
㉔雕 刻　diāokè
㉕出 自　chūzì
㉖高 超　gāochāo
㉗绝无仅有　juéwú jǐnyǒu
㉘刘备殿　Liú Bèi Diàn
㉙昭烈庙　Zhāoliè Miào
㉚赵 云　Zhào Yún
㉛黄 忠　Huáng Zhōng
㉜马 超　Mǎ Chāo
㉝仿 古　fǎnggǔ
㉞皮影戏　píyǐng xì
㉟吹面人　chuī miànrén
㊱中国结　Zhōngguó Jié
㊲盖碗茶　gàiwǎn chá
㊳变 脸　Biànliǎn
㊴吐 火　Tǔhuǒ
㊵顶 灯　Dǐngdēng
㊶休 闲　xiūxián

大的石碑。其中最大的一块石碑被称为"三绝碑"。这是因为这块碑上的文章、书法、雕刻都出自当时最著名的大师之手，水平高超，绝无仅有，所以叫"三绝碑"。这块石碑的文物价值特别高，是国家一级文物。

　　刘备殿，又叫昭烈庙，经过石碑就能看到，是纪念蜀国皇帝刘备的祠堂，再往后走看到的是诸葛亮殿，也就是"武侯祠"。武侯祠除了可以看到刘备、诸葛亮的塑像，还可以看到很多蜀国主要人物的塑像，比如关羽和张飞，还有五虎上将中的赵云、黄忠、马超。

　　武侯祠的旁边是锦里路。这是一条仿古的商业文化街，在这条街上人们可以看到很多有特色的民间艺术和手工艺品，比如皮影戏、剪纸、糖画、面人、中国结等。成都是一座美食之都，美食的种类非常丰富，而在锦里路上就能品尝到这些成都小吃和美食，对于"吃货"们来说，这可是一个好消息。锦里路还有很多四川特色餐厅和茶馆，人们可以在这里点上几杯盖碗茶，点上一桌地道的四川菜，一边品川茶吃川菜，一边欣赏川剧里的变脸、吐火、顶灯等精彩的演出，体验休闲舒适的成都慢生活。这就是历史与现代完美结合的"武侯祠"。

二、衣冠庙

①融 入　róngrù
②失 败　shībài
③悲 痛　bēitòng

　　在成都，除了武侯祠以外，其实还有很多三国遗迹已经融入成都人的日常生活之中，可能很多人每天都会说到、看到这些地名，从这些地方路过，但是却并不知道这些地名与三国历史之间的关系。比如衣冠庙，这是位于成都一环路上的一个地名，现在很多成都人说起衣冠庙，可能首先会想到衣冠庙地铁站。衣冠庙其实是与三国历史有关的一个重要遗迹。传说刘备的二弟关羽，在与吴国的战争中失败，被东吴人杀死。刘备听到这个消息以后悲痛伤心，因为他们两个人是桃园结义的好兄弟，一起经历过很多事情，关羽在被曹操抓住很多年都一直不愿意向曹操投降，最后千里走单骑，一个人骑着马过五关斩六将，克服各种困难才回到刘备的身边。可见他们两个人的感情非常深厚。关羽被杀时，蜀国与吴国还在打仗，所以刘备并没有找回关羽的尸首。按照中国古代的传统，如果一个很重要的人死了，人们会在埋葬他尸首的地方修建一座庙，后人就可以经常去祭拜他。

④ 投 降　tóuxiáng
⑤ 过五关斩六将
　　guò wǔguān zhǎn liùjiàng
⑥ 深 厚　shēnhòu
⑦ 尸 首　shīshǒu
⑧ 埋 葬　máizàng
⑨ 代 替　dàitì

　　可是如果没有关羽的尸首刘备怎么祭拜他呢？为了纪念自己的好兄弟关羽，刘备就在当初送关羽离开时两人分别的地方修了一座庙，塑了关羽的像，给这个塑像穿上了关羽生前爱穿的衣服，戴上他生前爱戴的帽子，在这个庙里祭拜关羽，表达他的悲痛之情。后来人们就把这个地方叫作"衣冠庙"，"衣"就是衣服，"冠"就是帽子。古代中国人在祭拜去世的人时有一个传统，如果找不到这个人的尸首，就用他生前穿过的衣服、戴过的帽子来代替他的尸首。这就是"衣冠庙"这个地名的来历。

三、洗面桥

　　衣冠庙附近还有一个和三国历史有关的遗迹，就是洗面桥。洗面桥与武侯祠东西相望，洗面桥的名字和衣冠庙也是有关系的。传说每次刘备去衣冠庙祭拜关羽的时候，都会在衣冠庙前的一条小河停下来，在河边洗一洗脸上的尘土，整理好自己的衣服，再进衣冠庙祭拜，以表示对关羽的尊重。在这条小河上有一座石板桥，刘备每次去祭拜关羽时都会在这座桥下的河边洗脸，所以人们就把这座桥叫作"洗面桥"。在古汉语中把"脸"叫作"面"，因此"洗脸"就是"洗面"。今天的成都洗面桥是一座现代街区广场，还有一座新建的仿古石桥，是用青石做的，宽约两米，长约三米，在桥的石板上雕刻着三国故事的场景。

① 尘 土　chéntǔ
② 整 理　zhěnglǐ
③ 表 示　biǎoshì
④ 尊 重　zūnzhòng
⑤ 青 石　qīngshí

四、三义庙 三圣祠 三圣乡

① 巧 合　　qiǎohé
② 经 历　　jīnglì
③ 不离不弃　bùlí-bùqì
④ 情 义　　qíngyì
⑤ 康 熙　　Kāng Xī
⑥ 提督街　　Tídū Jiē
⑦ 顺 便　　shùnbiàn
⑧ 宋 代　　Sòngdài
⑨ 龙泉驿　　Lóngquányì
⑩ 拜 谒　　bàiyè
⑪ 氛 围　　fēnwéi
⑫ 民 俗　　mínsú
⑬ 祈 求　　qíqiú
⑭ 隆 重　　lóngzhòng
⑮ 壮 观　　zhuàngguān
⑯ 独一无二　dúyī-wúèr

在成都市还有几个带"三"的地名都与三国历史关系密切。这好像是一种巧合，其实主要是和三国故事中著名的"桃园三结义"有关。刘备、关羽、张飞三个人在一座桃花园中结拜为兄弟，从此之后，三个人始终互相信任、互相支持，一起出生入死、经历种种危险、克服重重困难，最终成功地建立了蜀国。三个人这种不离不弃的兄弟情义让所有人感动、敬佩，所以清代康熙初年专门在成都市的提督街修建了三义庙来纪念他们，1998 年由于城市建设的需要，三义庙被搬到了现在的武侯祠里。所以现在人们在参观完武侯祠以后顺便就可以参观三义庙了。

如果人们是在春节期间游玩成都，那一定不要错过成都一年一度盛大的民俗活动：大庙会。而大庙会就是在三义庙前举行的。大庙会中最重要的活动是在大年初一的早晨"游喜神方"。从宋代开始，每到春节，成都人就有出南门"游喜神方"的习俗，就是来到位于成都南边的武侯祠，拜谒刘备、关羽、张飞和诸葛亮。因为他们都是四川人心中的英雄，被四川人看成是忠、义、财神，合称为"喜神"。"游喜神方"就是来到喜神所在的方位，祈求一年平安吉祥。大年初一早上，演员们穿上古装扮演刘备、关羽、张飞、诸葛亮等重要人物，在三义庙前举行仿古祭祀活动，场面热闹壮观，所以如果不想错过这独一无二的文化体验，初一早上就千万别睡懒觉，早早地到武侯祠的三义庙前等候，去感受浓浓的三国历史氛围。除了初一早上的"游喜神方"，春节期间在三义庙以及武侯祠、锦里还会举行各式各样的民俗活动和文艺表演，从早上一直到深夜，绝对可以让游人一饱眼福、一饱耳福、一饱口福！

除了三义庙以外，过去成都还有一个很有名的纪念刘备、关羽、张飞三人的祠庙，叫三圣祠，位于现在成都的青年路附近，过去很多人也到三圣祠去祭拜、怀念刘关张三人，人们还在三圣祠附近修建了一个三义宫，也是因这三个人而得名。三义宫曾经还是老成都有名的一个剧场，很多川剧大师都在那里演出过。现在三圣祠、三义宫都没有了，只留下了三圣祠这个街名。

　　说到三国，说到刘关张，不得不说的还有三圣乡。三圣乡在成都市的东南方。三圣乡因那里过去有个三圣庙而得名。那里的三圣庙是清代建起的，最开始供奉的是中国历史上著名的三位圣贤：为人民尝百草、教会中国人掌握农业技术的神农氏；华夏民族的祖先——黄帝；创造汉字的仓颉。但后来这个三圣庙改成供奉刘备、关羽和张飞三人了，这也许能说明刘关张三人在成都人心目中的地位是多么重要。现在的三圣乡已经成为成都有名的风景旅游区，是国家 AAAA 级旅游景区，里面有"荷塘月色""幸福梅林"等主题景点，人们一年四季都可以在三圣乡体验不同风格和特色的美景。而且三圣乡由于种植各种花卉，有各种以花卉为主题的景点，已经被成都人称为"三圣花乡"了。

　　三国时代是中国历史上一个非常重要的时期，在这个时期发生了很多经典的历史故事，也出现了很多著名的英雄人物，直到今天人们都还在谈论这些故事，还在纪念那些英雄。三国历史对中国文化有着巨大的影响，在唐诗宋词里留下了很多传唱千年的诗句，小说《三国演义》成为中国四大名著之一，中国的国粹京剧中也有很多有关三国故事的经典剧目，汉语中也能找到很多有三国历史典故的成语、俗语。三国给中华文化留下了一笔巨大的财富，我们应该好好地去学习它、了解它，再把三国的传奇故事带到全世界去，为更多人打开一扇了解中国文化的窗户。

⑰供　奉　　gòngfèng
⑱神农氏　　Shénnóngshì
⑲黄　帝　　Huángdì
⑳花　卉　　huāhuì

①经典　　　jīngdiǎn
②谈论　　　tánlùn
③唐诗宋词　Tángshī Sòngcí
④四大名著　Sìdà Míngzhù
⑤国粹　　　guócuì
⑥京剧　　　Jīngjù
⑦剧目　　　jùmù
⑧典故　　　diǎngù

Ma Lan: The Three Kingdoms culture deeply fascinates me. My mind is filled with its stories and heroes.

Wen Xiaoxi: Absolutely, I feel the same. What a shame that we were not born at that time and cannot experience these heroes'elegant demeanor for ourselves. If only we could go back in time!

Lin Chuan: If we could go back in time, I'd definitely go look for Zhuge Liang. I admire him the most and there's so much I want to ask him. Even if I could only be his servant bringing tea and pouring water, I'd be more than willing.

Jiang Yihua: If I could go back, I'd look for Guan Yu. I must see for myself whether the real Guan Yu has the same red face and magnificent beard as he does in the legends. I also want to look for Zhou Cang, who cares for Guan Yu's blade, and let me try out Guan Yu's big blade. If I post a photo of Guan Yu and me holding the Green Dragon Crescent Blade to WeChat Moments, a lot of people will definitely envy me.

Teacher: Your imagination really runs wild. Your time-traversing dreams don't have to remain dreams, though. I know a place where you can fulfill your dream of going back in time.

Wen Xiaoxi: Really now? Where is this place? I can't wait to go there!

Teacher: This place is seemingly far away, but actually close at hand – Chengdu.

Lin Chuan: You're joking, right? Chengdu is such a modern city; where would there be any traces of Three Kingdoms history?

Teacher: Among China's big cities, Chengdu is a place that preservers an abundance of historical remains of the Three Kingdoms era. According to a survey conducted by experts in archeology, history and museology, there are 46 sites in total in the Chengdu area.

Jiang Yihua: 46? So many? Incredible! Who would've thought that Three Kingdoms history was right in front of my eyes all along!

Teacher: Yes! You could say that Chengdu is one large lively exhibition hall of historical relics belonging to the Three Kingdoms. Perhaps when you walk through a street, enter a subway station, stay in a park or live in a home community, all of them contain the stories and legends of the Three Kingdoms. Today, we are going to visit several of the most famous Three Kingdoms sites in Chengdu, so that you can touch, see and experience Three Kingdoms culture for yourself and get to know the elegant demeanor of those famous Three Kingdoms characters.

All students: Wonderful! Let's go right away!

Teacher: All right. Our time travel to the Three Kingdoms is starting right away.

In the Three Kingdoms era, the capital of Shu was Sichuan's Chengdu, which is home to many historical sites of the former state to this very day. Entering these sites feels like entering a living period of history, as if you were personally present during that time, experiencing the places where once the figures of the Three Kingdoms walked. These sites are about 2,000 years old and quietly tell enchanting, epic stories, closing the gap between the present and the past, letting the Three Kingdoms period be within reach.

If you want to learn more about the history of Shu, you definitely cannot miss out on visiting Chengdu.

[Part 1] Wuhou Temple
If you go to Chengdu, there is a Three Kingdoms site you must visit. This place is called Wuhou Temple. If you go to Chengdu but do not go to Wuhou Temple, it would be the same as going to Beijing and not to the Forbidden City or going to Shanghai and not to the Bund: it will fill you with regret. Wuhou Temple was built in commemoration of Zhuge Liang. He helped Liu Bei manage Shu in Chengdu and did a lot of good things for the Chengdu people. In memory of his tremendous contribution to Chengdu, a memorial hall in his honor was built after his death. Zhuge Liang was once conferred the title of "Wuxiang Hou" and received the posthumous title of "Zhongwu Hou". This is why the temple to commemorate him was later called "Wuhou Temple".

Its other unique feature lies in being China's only memorial temple for both monarchs and ministers to be jointly worshipped. In ancient China, there was a huge difference in status between the emperor and his ministers. There was no way one could jointly offer sacrifices for the emperor and his ministers. Since Zhuge Liang's contributions to Shu were great in number and far-reaching in effect, he has enjoyed the privilege to receive worship in the same ancestral temple as emperor Liu Bei. He is the only person in Chinese history to enjoy such treatment. It is evident that Zhuge Liang shaped Shu greatly.

Wuhou Temple is located in the south of Chengdu. Famous Tang Dynasty poet Du Fu once described the temple in a poem, "Where lies the shrine commemorating the renowned Premier of Shu? On the outside, [where] the City of the Brocade Officer is surrounded with groves of cypress trees." (The Premier of Shu)"The City of the Brocade Officer" is another name for Chengdu, as is "The City of Hibiscus" because in ancient times, hibiscus flowers could be found everywhere in Chengdu and were the city's official flower. Therefore, Chengdu was called "The City of Hibiscus".

Wuhou Temple was first built in 223 AD. In its history of more than 1,000 years, it was destroyed and rebuilt several times. Its main building, as can be seen today, was rebuilt in 1672 during the Qing Dynasty. The entire grounds span an area of 150,000 square meters and mainly consist of three parts: the cultural relics area, the botanical garden area and Jinli.

The most important historical sites and cultural relics of Wuhou Temple are located in the cultural relics area. As soon as you pass the gate of Wuhou Temple, you will first see six tall stone tablets to your sides, and the tallest one is known as "Sanjuebei" (Stone of Triple Perfection). This is because the writings, calligraphy and carvings on this tablet stem from the hands of the back then most famous great masters and are incredible artistic feats that cannot be found anywhere else. The cultural value of this stone is particularly high and counts among China's first-class cultural relics.

The Temple of Liu Bei, also known as Zhaolie Temple, can be seen past the tablets and is the ancestry hall built in commemoration of Liu Bei, Emperor of Shu. Going further back, you will see the Temple of Zhuge Liang, or "Wuhou Temple". Apart from Liu Bei and Zhuge Liang, you can see a lot of statues of other main figures of the Three Kingdoms, such as Guan Yu and Zhang Fei, in Wuhou Temple. The other three statues of these "Five Tiger Generals" that can also be seen are Zhao Yun, Huang Zhong and Ma Chao.

Next to Wuhou Temple is Jinli Road. This is an archaized commercial and cultural street where you can see a lot of unique folk art and handicrafts, such as shadow play, papercutting, sugar paintings, dough figurines, traditional Chinese knots, and so on. Chengdu is a city of delicacies and boasts a wide range of all delicious foods. In Jinli Road, you can enjoy these snacks and delicacies. For "foodies", this should be great news. Jinli Road also has many Sichuan restaurants and teahouses where you can order gaiwan tea and authentic Sichuan food. While you savor tea and food, you may enjoy Sichuan opera's exciting acts of face-changing, fire-spitting and lamp-rolling. You will experience the slow-paced and leisurely lifestyle in Chengdu for yourself. This is the perfect combination of history and modernity that can be found at Wuhou Temple.

[Part 2] Yiguan Temple

Apart from Wuhou Temple, there are many other Three Kingdoms sites that have become part of daily life in Chengdu. A lot of people may talk about or see their names or pass by them, but do not know in the slightest what is the connection between these names and Three Kingdoms history. Yiguan Temple is such an example: it is a place name that can be found on Chengdu's First Ring Road. Talking about Yiguan Temple, many Chengdu people may first think of the Yiguan Temple metro station. In fact, Yiguan Temple is an important Three Kingdoms relic. Legend has it that Liu Bei's second brother Guan Yu suffered defeat in the war with Wu and was killed by Wu forces. Liu Bei was heartbroken when he heard the news, because the two of them were brothers who took an oath in the Peach Garden and had been together through a lot. Guan Yu was held captive by Cao Cao for many years and was reluctant to surrender. Finally, Guan Yu rode alone for thousand miles, crossed five passes and slew six generals, overcoming all kinds of difficulties before returning to Liu Bei's side. Their deep emotional bond is evident. When Guan Yu was killed, Shu and Wu were still at war, so Liu Bei did not retrieve Guan Yu's corpse. According to ancient Chinese tradition, if an important person died, a temple would be built where this person was buried, and later generations may frequent this place for worship.

However, if there is no corpse, how would Liu Bei go about worshipping Guan Yu? In commemoration of his good brother Guan Yu, Liu Bei built a temple at the place where the two of them went separate ways. He made a statue in Guan Yu's likeness, dressed it in the clothes Guan Yu loved to wear during his lifetime and placed his favorite hat on its head. It was in that temple that Liu Bei worshipped Guan Yu to express his grief. Later, this place was called "Yiguan Temple", where "yi" stands for "clothes" and "guan" for "hat". The ancient Chinese had a tradition of worshipping those who died: if their corpses could not be found, their clothes and hats, which they used to wear before their death, would replace their corpses. This is the origin of the place named "Yiguan Temple".

[Part 3] Ximian Bridge

There is another site linked to the Three Kingdoms close to Yiguan Temple: Ximian Bridge. Ximian Bridge and Wuhou Temple are situated east and west across each other. Ximian Bridge's name relates to Yiguan Temple. According to the legend, every time Liu Bei went to Yiguan Temple to worship Guan Yu, he would first stop at a small river before Yiguan Temple where he would wash the dust from his face and fix his clothing, and then enter Yiguan Temple, in order to express his respect towards Guan Yu. There is a stone bridge on this river, under which Liu Bei washed his face every time he was on his way to Yiguan Temple. As a result, this bridge was called "Ximian Bridge". In ancient Chinese, "mian" instead "lian" is the word for "face", so "ximian" refers to "face-washing". Today's Ximian Bridge is a modern square that also boasts a newly built bridge in the style of the ancients, which is made of bluestone. It is about two meters wide and three meters long. There are scenes of the Three Kingdoms stories carved on the stone slabs of the bridge.

[Part 4] Sanyi Temple / Sansheng Temple / Sansheng Village

In Chengdu, there are several other places with "three" in their names that are related to Three Kingdoms history. What seems to be a coincidence is actually connected to the famous "Oath of the Peach Garden". Since Liu Bei, Guan Yu and Zhang Fei became sworn brothers in a peach garden, these three people always trusted and supported each other. They went through fire and water, experiencing various dangers and overcoming arduous challenges, and finally succeeded in establishing Shu. These three people who always stood by each other represent comradeship both touching and admirable, which is why Early Qing Emperor Kangxi specially had three temples built in their commemoration in Chengdu. In 1998, due to urban construction needs, Sanyi Temple was moved inside the present Wuhou Temple. As a result, you can conveniently visit Sanyi Temple after you have been to Wuhou Temple.

If you travel to Chengdu during the Spring Festival, you cannot miss the grand folk festival held once a year in Chengdu: the Great Temple Fair, which is held in front of Sanyi Temple. The fair's most important event is the "God of Happiness Parade". Starting from the Song Dynasty, the people of Chengdu have upheld this tradition every Spring Festival. They go to Wuhou Temple, which is in Chengdu's South, and pay homage to Liu Bei, Guan Yu, Zhang Fei and Zhuge Liang. Since they are heroes in the hearts of the Sichuanese, they are considered the epitome of loyalty, righteousness and wealth, and collectively called the "God of Happiness". During the "God of Happiness Parade", participants go to this god's places and pray for a year of good luck. In the early morning of New Year's Day, actors wear ancient costumes dressing up as Liu Bei, Guan Yu, Zhang Fei and Zhuge Liang to hold sacrificial ceremonies in the style of the ancients in front of Sanyi Temple. The scene is lively and spectacular, so if you do not want to miss this unique cultural experience, do not sleep in, and go early to the front of Sanyi Temple inside Wuhou Temple, waiting for the event to unfold. You will feel immersed in Three Kingdoms history. Other than the parade on New Year's Day, a wide range of folk activities and artistic performances will be held in Sanyi Temple, Wuhou Temple and Jinli during the Spring Festival. Any visitors are sure to feast their eyes, ears and palates on excitement abound from early morning to late in the night.

Apart from Sanyi Temple, there is another ancestral temple built in commemoration of Liu Bei, Guan Yu and Zhang Fei, called Sansheng Temple, which is located close to Qingnian Road. A lot of people passing by go to Sansheng Temple for worship and commemoration of Liu Bei, Guan Yu and Zhang Fei. Sanyi Palace was built close to Sanyi Temple and is also named after these three personages. Sanyi Palace used to be a famous theater in Old Chengdu, where many a Sichuan Opera master performed. Nowadays, Sansheng Temple and Sanyi Palace are long gone and only the street name of Sansheng Temple remains.

You cannot talk about the Three Kingdoms and Liu Bei, Guan Yu and Zhang Fei without mentioning Sansheng Village. Sansheng Village is situated in Chengdu's southeast. Sansheng Village was named after the Sansheng Temple located there.

The Sansheng Temple there was built in the Qing Dynasty. Initially, this temple was devoted to the three famous saints in Chinese history: Shennong, who tried all kinds of flora and taught the Chinese the practices of agriculture; the Yellow Emperor, who is the ancestor of the Chinese nation; and Cang Jie, the creator of Chinese characters. However, this Sansheng Temple later was designated to enshrine Liu Bei, Guan Yu and Zhang Fei, which may go to show the importance of these three personages in the eyes of the people in Chengdu. Today, Sansheng Village has turned into a famous scenic tourist area in Chengdu and is a national AAAA tourist attraction, boasting themed attractions such as "Lotus Pond Moonlight" and "Happy Plum Forest". Visitors to Sansheng Village can experience beautiful sceneries with their own charm and unique features all year round. As various flowers are planted in Sansheng Village, there are all kinds of attractions that are flower-themed, and Chengdu people call Sansheng Village "Sansheng Flower Village".

The Three Kingdoms era was a very important period in Chinese history, during which many classic historical stories took place and many famous heroic figures emerged. People talk about these stories and honor these heroes to this very day. The history of the Three Kingdoms has had a tremendous influence on Chinese culture: it inspired Tang and Song poets to write verses that have been passed on through the ages; the *Romance of the Three Kingdoms* is one of the four classic Chinese novels; many Three Kingdoms stories are part of the classical repertoire of traditional Beijing opera; and you may find a large number of set phrases and proverbs from classical stories set in the Three Kingdoms in the Chinese language. The Three Kingdoms is one gigantic treasure trove, which we should study and understand well, and then carry the legends out into the world, to help other countries open a window into Chinese culture.

词语

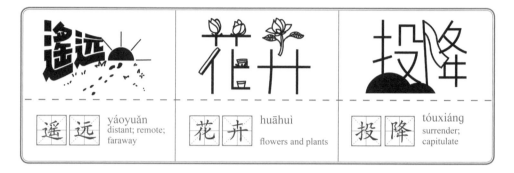

遥 远	yáoyuǎn distant; remote; faraway	
花 卉	huāhuì flowers and plants	
投 降	tóuxiáng surrender; capitulate	

zháo mí 着 迷	be fascinated/ captivated	jiàn shi 见 识	enrich one's experience
fēng cǎi 风 采	elegant demeanor	chuān yuè 穿 越	pass through; cut across; here: go back through time
pèi fú 佩 服	admire	qīn yǎn 亲 眼	with one's own eyes; personally
tiān fāng yè tán 天 方 夜 谭	Arabian Nights; fantasy story	pò bù jí dài 迫 不 及 待	too impatient to wait; itching to get on with it
bù kě sī yì 不 可 思 议	inconceivable; unimaginable; unthinkable	huó shēng shēng 活 生 生	real; living; vivid; lively
zǒu fǎng 走 访	visit; go and see	qīn zì 亲 自	personally; in person; oneself

chù mō 触　摸	touch; feel
yǐn rén rù shèng 引 人 入 胜	fascinating; enchanting; bewitching; thrilling
cuò guò 错　过	miss; let slip
gòng xiàn 贡　献	contribute; devote
zhuī shì 追　谥	confer a posthumous name or title
jì sì 祭　祀	offer sacrifices (to gods or ancestors)
dài yù 待　遇	treatment
pò huài 破　坏	destroy; wreck; obliterate; do great damage to; disrupt
wén wù 文　物	cultural relic
diāo kè 雕　刻	carving; engraving

shēn lín qí jìng 身 临 其 境	be personally on the scene; be present on the scene; fully immersed
bō lán zhuàng kuò 波 澜 壮 阔	unfolding on a magnificent scale
jì niàn 纪　念	commemorate
fēng 封	confer (a title, territory, etc.) upon
cí táng 祠　堂	ancestral hall/temple; memorial temple
xuán shū 悬　殊	(great) disparity; wide gap
bǎi shù 柏　树	cypress tree
zhǔ tǐ 主　体	main body/part
shí bēi 石　碑	stone tablet; stele
chū zì 出　自	come from; originate from; stem from

gāo chāo 高 超	superb; excellent
fǎng gǔ 仿 古	modelled after an antique; in the style of the ancients; archaize
róng rù 融 入	integrate into
bēi tòng 悲 痛	grieve; sorrow
shī shǒu 尸 首	dead body of a human being; corpse
dài tì 代 替	replace; substitute for; take the place of
zhěng lǐ 整 理	put in order; straighten out; arrange; sort out; fix (clothing···)
zūn zhòng 尊 重	respect; value; esteem
qiǎo hé 巧 合	coincidence
bù lí bù qì 不 离 不 弃	stand by; steadfast loyalty

jué wú jǐn yǒu 绝 无 仅 有	only one of its kind; unique
xiū xián 休 闲	leisure
shī bài 失 败	be defeated; lose (a war, etc.)
shēn hòu 深 厚	deep; profound
mái zàng 埋 葬	bury (the dead)
chén tǔ 尘 土	dust
biǎo shì 表 示	show; express; indicate
qīng shí 青 石	bluestone
jīng lì 经 历	experience; go through
qíng yì 情 义	affection; ties of friendship, comradeship, etc.

shùn biàn 顺 便	in passing; conveniently
fēn wéi 氛 围	atmosphere
qí qiú 祈 求	pray for
zhuàngguān 壮 观	magnificent; spectacular
gòng fèng 供 奉	enshrine and worship
jīng diǎn 经 典	classics
guó cuì 国 粹	quintessence of national (here: Chinese) culture
guò wǔ guān 过 五 关 zhǎn liù jiàng 斩 六 将	cross five passes and slay six gen- erals; surmount all difficulties (on the way to success)

bài yè 拜 谒	pay a formal visit; call to pay respects; pay homage; honor
mín sú 民 俗	folk custom
lóng zhòng 隆 重	grand; solemn; ceremonious
dú yī wú èr 独 一 无 二	unique; unparalleled; unmatched; unrivaled
zhòng zhí 种 植	plant; grow
tán lùn 谈 论	discuss; talk about
jù mù 剧 目	repertoire; program; list of plays or operas
diǎn gù 典 故	classical story

专有名词

1. 周仓　　　/ Zhōu Cāng / Zhou Cang (Guan Yu's fictional weapon bearer)

2. 青龙偃　　/Qīnglóng Yǎnyuè Dāo/ the Green Dragon Crescent Blade (Guan Yu's legendary
　月刀　　　weapon in " Romance of the Three Kingdoms") Materia Medica

3. 杜甫　　　/ Dù Fǔ / Du Fu (712-770); prominent Tang poet; the greatest of the Chinese
　　　　　　poets along with Li Bai

4. 锦官城　　/ Jǐnguān Chéng / City of the Brocade Officer (alternative name for Cheng-du)

5. 蓉城　　　/ Róng Chéng / City of Hibiscus (alternative name for Chengdu)

6. 清朝　　　/ Qīngcháo / Qing Dynasty (1644-1911)

7. 刘备殿　　/ Liú Bèi Diàn / Temple of Liu Bei

8. 昭烈庙　　/ Zhāoliè Miào / Zhaolie Temple

9. 五虎上将　/ Wǔhǔ Shàngjiàng / the Five Tiger Generals (usually refers to the five best
　　　　　　military generals serving under a ruler; not a term that is used officially or found
　　　　　　in historical records; in the Three Kingdoms period, these five generals refer to
　　　　　　Shu Han's Guan Yu, Zhang Fei, Zhao Yun, Ma Chao and Huang Zhong)

10. 赵云　/ Zhào Yún / Zhao Yun

11. 黄忠　/ Huáng Zhōng / Huang Zhong

12. 马超　/ Mǎ Chāo / Ma Chao

13. 康熙　/ Kāng Xī / Kangxi (1661-1722), title of the reign of Aisin-Gioro Xuanye (爱新觉罗·玄烨), 4th emperor of the Qing Dynasty

14. 提督街　/ Tídū Jiē / Tidu Street (Provincial Military Commander Street); title of a high military official in the Chinese provinces of Qing Dynasty (1644-1911)

15. 宋代　/ Sòngdài / Song Dynasty

16. 龙泉驿　/ Lóngquányì / Longquanyi (district of Chengdu city)

17. 神农氏　/ Shénnóngshì /Shennong, or Farmer God (ca. 2000 BC); creator of agriculture in China

18. 黄帝　/ Huángdì / Yellow Emperor, legendary ruler of China and ancestor of the Chinese people, reigned ca. 2697-2597 BC

19. 仓颉　/ Cāng Jié / Cang Jie, legendary scribe of the Yellow Emperor and creator of Chinese writing

近义词

1. 纪念 — 怀念 jìniàn-huáiniàn
2. 祭祀 — 祭拜 jìsì - jìbài
3. 遗迹 — 古迹 yíjì - gǔjì
4. 风景 — 景区 — 景点 fēngjǐng - jǐngqū - jǐngdiǎn

俗语

Yuǎn zài tiān biān jìn zài yǎn qián 远 在 天 边 近在眼 前	seemingly far away, actually close at hand (said playfully to call attention to sb. or sth. right in front of sb.'s eyes)

语言点

1. 为……而……
2. 被……称为……
3. 对……来说
4. 重（如重修、重建）
5. 按照……的传统（规定、规矩、习俗、风俗等）
6. 一饱……福（如一饱眼福、一饱口福、一饱耳福）

思 考

1. 你能说一说"武侯祠"名字的来历吗？

2. 成都还有哪些别名？

3. 武侯祠由哪几个部分组成？

4. "衣冠庙"这个地名是怎么来的呢？

5. 请问在中国祭拜、纪念去世的亲人或者朋友有一些什么样的传统风俗和节日？在你们国家，有什么样的传统风俗和节日？

6. 刘备每次去祭拜关羽以前要做些什么？

7. 春节期间，三义庙前会举行什么活动？

8. 除了三义庙，以前的成都人还去哪儿祭拜刘备、关羽和张飞？

9. 三圣乡现在是一个什么样的地方？

参考文献
[References]

[1] 吕思勉 . 三国史话 [M]. 北京：中华书局，2009.

[2] 易中天 . 品三国 [M]. 上海：上海文艺出版社，2007.

[3] 赵玉平 . 向诸葛亮借智慧 [M]. 北京：电子工业出版社，2011.

[4] 梅铮铮 . 忠义春秋 —— 关公崇拜与民族文化心理 [M]. 成都：四川人民出版社，1994.

[5] 袁庭栋 . 成都街巷志 [M]. 成都：四川教育出版社，2010.

[6] 成都及附近三国文化遗迹知多少 [EB/OL]. http://blog.sina.com.cn/s/blog_4cc0be890102wfvi.html.

[7] 三国遗址遗迹今何在 [EB/OL].http://www.sohu.com/a/113901615_115553.

图书在版编目（CIP）数据

成都印象／西南财经大学 汉语国际推广成都基地著 —成都：西南财经
大学出版社，2019.7
（走进天府系列教材）
ISBN 987-7-5504-3776-0

Ⅰ．①成… Ⅱ．①西… Ⅲ．①汉语—对外汉语教学—教材②成都—
概况 Ⅳ．①H 195.4②K 927.11
中国版本图书馆 CIP 数据核字（2018）第 241717 号

走进天府系列教材：成都印象·梦三国之蜀国

ZOUJIN TIANFU XILIE JIAOCAI:CHENGDU YINXIANG·MENG SANGUO ZHI SHUGUO

西南财经大学 汉语国际推广成都基地 著

策 划：王正好 何春梅
责任编辑：李 才
装帧设计：张艳洁
插 画：辣点设计
责任印制：朱曼丽

出版发行	西南财经大学出版社（四川省成都市光华村街 55 号）
网 址	http://www.bookcj.com
电子邮件	bookcj@ foxmail.com
邮政编码	610074
电 话	028-87353785
照 排	上海辣点广告设计咨询有限公司
印 刷	四川新财印务有限公司
成品尺寸	170mm×240mm
印 张	46.5
字 数	875 千字
版 次	2019 年 7 月第 1 版
印 次	2019 年 7 月第 1 次印刷
印 数	1-2050 套
书 号	ISBN 978-7-5504-3776-0
定 价	198.00 元（套）